Unconditional praise

Erika Parkman

faith books & MORE

Suwanee, GA

First published by Faith Books & MORE
978-0-9852729-0-6

Printed in the United States of America.

This book is printed on acid-free paper.

faith books&MORE

3255 Lawrenceville-Suwanee Rd.
Suite P250
Suwanee, GA 30024
publishing@faithbooksandmore.com
www.faithbooksandmore.com

DEDICATION

This book is dedicated to the Trinity. The Father, the Son and the Holy Spirit.

Thank you for loving me and keeping me safe in your hands. I have truly lived
(John 10:29 KJV)

"My father, which gave them me, is greater than all; and no man is able to pluck them out of my father's hand". Lord even though the thief whom I have found to be the devil came to kill (R.I.P.) My daughter Trinity C. Parkman he tried to steal my sanity and my joy and he destroy my marriage. Lord none of these things has plucked me from your hands. I love you and I dedication not only this first fruit but all to you. I am truly thankful and grateful that I have an intimate relationship with you that is everlasting and filled with unconditional un-wavered love and praise to you.

ACKNOWLEDGMENTS

I would first like to thank the Trinity the father, son and holy ghost. Thank you for protecting, guiding and dying for me, you have set me up for such an appointed time as this with a divine appointed purpose that I will faithfully fully do, thank you from your humble servant Erika Parkman

I would like to thank my pastor's Creflo and Taffi Dollar; you have made a mark in my life that just can't be erased. Thank you for imparting the knowledge, wisdom and word of God in my spirit which has turned into physical manifestation. Because you have taught me the word of God with simplicity and understanding which I was able to apply in my everyday life thank you with love.

My parents Arthur R. Parkman and Phyllis J. Parkman I love you both more than words can say. I thank you and give you honor this day. Even though times was trying I am happy to know that I still have parents whom always imparted God in my life whether you are together or apart. To my father personally, thank you for not letting your hold up, I can truly appreciate your rule of an iron fist, may god bless you without measure.

To my mother personally, do you remember when you told me the first shall be last and the last shall be first. Yes, I am your last child out of five children but you told me this because you saw, I was peculiar thank you for letting me come to Atlanta and trusting God would take care of me at the age of 19, thank you for all your prayers, longsuffering and love and wisdom that is priceless. God gave you to me and I am forever grateful that God gave me you to be my mother. You have ruled our home always with Love and an abundance of patience and integrity.

To my siblings Melissa, Arthur ray Jr., Wendy, and Kimberly. I am glad to have you all in my life, may our bond as sister and brother grow stronger. If we never had much we always had each other and prayer I love each one of you unconditionally.

To my Grandparents Mr. and Mrs. Curry, your strength, wisdom, support, and love have helped carry me a long way. To my grandmother Mrs. Curry thank you for your prayers and words of encouragement, this is the only woman I know that is like ivory soap, you can push her under water but she will always float back up to the top.

Thank you for letting me know that god took that same pattern that you are from and cut me out as well. Granddaddy you are one man with a pure heart and this shall be rewarded. Thank you both with love

To Pastor Barber Tarver my spiritual mother, thank you for your wisdom and never giving up on me. You are one of the strong women in my life. I know God sent you in my life and you have sown seeds within me that I will never forget or cast away, thank you with love and much gratitude.

TABLE OF CONTENTS

INTRODUCTION

God loves us all unconditionally. So why should god have to give you something for you to praise him unconditionally? We know how mighty God is and there is nothing too hard for God, if you don't know or you are unsure by the time you finish this book you will know of his might and power, it is in his word that one must taste and see.

When you pray and worship God for that very thing that you need or want and desire when he is silent and does not answer. This tells whether you are a Fan or a Follower. When you choose God and his son, you must lose your own life to gain life. Submitting to the Lord no matter what is going on and how hard it gets, the unconditional praise and worshipper, must praise god in spirit and in truth, do a self-evaluation and check your own motives.

We want god to supply us and answer our prayers, why would God increase you more when you have not even praised him for what he has already done. If we are faithful over the little, he will entrust us with more, even when we don't praise and worship him like we should he still helps us out of his unconditional love, how should we approach the presence of God? With praise and with the right motives. When you have the correct motives, nothing will move you off your praise and worship to God.

So I ask you today, what is your motive for praising and worship to GOD, if you are unsure keep reading.

I pray in the name of Jesus and by the blood of Jesus, each and every time you read this book, revelation knowledge will flow without hindrance from the enemy or any other source of demonic forces. The word of God says that we trend over all the power of the enemy and I walk in my dominion now. Lord I pray let the words come off the pages and penetrate hearts, lord let the Holy Spirit fall upon the person reading this book, lord this is nothing about me but all about you. Lord let men, women, children and sinners fall on their face suddenly giving you all the worship, praise, honor and the glory in Jesus name
Amen.

Chapter

1

spirit & truth

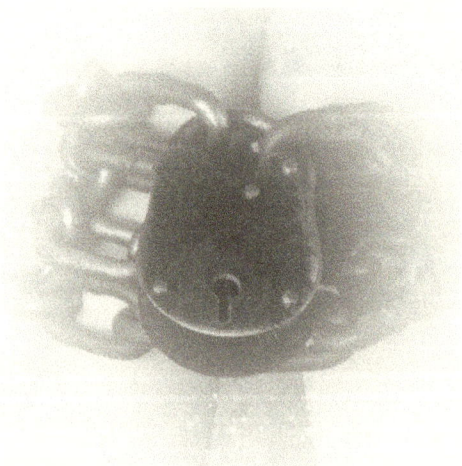

> "But the hour cometh and now is, when the true worshippers shall worship the Father in spirit and in truth: for the Father seeketh such to worship him. God is a Spirit: and they that worship him must worship him in spirit and in truth" (John 4: 23-24).

We must remember that God is a spirit being.

At this point, you may be thinking, "Yes, worship and praise," and by the illustration on the cover you may be wondering how someone can praise God while they are bound. Many Christians today actually have this problem: They try to seek and praise God, but they are hindered by the chains of doubt and distrust. There is another level of praise that God thirsts for – one of unconditional praise in spirit and in truth.

You may be confused (or maybe even offended). You may be wondering, "How can this woman judge another's praise?" But this is not coming from me; God has placed this upon my heart, and I would like to help you understand what it means to praise Him in spirit and in truth as Scripture directs.

Have you ever fervently praised God in Jesus' name, yet He seemed to remain silent? If you have, you should continue reading.

Delight yourself in the Lord.

Unconditional praise

Unconditional – *without conditions or limitations, not limited by conditions (Webster's Dictionary).*

Conditional – *qualified by reservation, imposing, containing, subject to or depending on a condition or set of conditions; not absolute; made or allowed on certain terms (Webster's Dictionary).* I often tell people, "You can lie to me, but there are two people in this world to which you can never successfully lie: yourself and God." How many times have you begun to pray or praise or worship God because He paid your power bill? You know the truth and so does He; were you praising Him out of love for Who He is, or do you love Him simply because of what He does for you? Ponder that for a few moments, but continue to read.

Praise – *to glorify, especially by attribution or perfections (Webster's Dictionary).*

So what would cause you to praise Him whether He pays the electric bill, the mortgage, the rent, the car note, or not?

Unconditional praise

let everything that hath breath praise the Lord

Conditional Probability *is the probability that an event will occur, given that one or more other events have already occurred (Webster's Dictionary).*

Does your praise and worship fall into one of the above categories? Do you have unconditional praise, conditional praise, or conditional probability praise? I can tell you now that God is looking for people who will praise Him no matter what pit, fire, bondage or sickness they are in. By the way, He delivered us from all of the above when He died for us. He loves us whether or not we love Him, and don't let anyone make you believe differently.

"Forever, O Lord, thy word is settled in heaven" (Psalm 119:89, KJV). *This passage tells us that the God's word is settled, so we should do what His word says and trust that it is steadfast.*

"So shall my word be that goeth forth out of my mouth: it shall not return unto me void, but is shall accomplish that which I please, and it shall prosper in the thing whereto I sent it" (Isaiah 55:11, KJV).

English lesson 101: "Not" means "unlikely," "no" or "not happening," and "but" means, "forget everything before the 'but;' this is what I really want to say." Okay, so you have all these promises in God's Word, and you still give Him conditional probability praise after He said to praise Him in spirit and truth? You may want to check your faith.

Unconditional praise

"Be careful for nothing; but in everything by prayer and supplication with thanksgiving let your request be known unto God. And the peace of God, which passeth all understanding, shall keep your hearts and minds through Christ Jesus" (Philippians 4:6-7, KJV).

"Be not ye therefore like unto them; for your Father knoweth what things ye have need of, before ye ask him" (Matthew 6:8 KJV).

In these few but important verses, the Lord has said that He is already going to do what we ask and give us what we need. So what makes you think that He does not know what you need and even pleasurable things you want?

"Before I formed thee in the belly I knew thee; and before thou camest forth out the womb I sanctified thee" (Jeremiah 1:5 KJV). So why do you give God pitiful worship and praise while He already knows exactly what you want and need? We need to stop going off of what others say and read it for ourselves. *"Study and be eager and do your utmost to present yourself to God*

approved" (2 Timothy 2:15, Amp). In other words, read His Word and find out what He has said about you and to you.

Have you ever been in love? After a first date, if you happened to speak to that special someone's best friend, what is the first thing you would ask? It was probably something like, "What did he say about me?" And if their answer was positive, it would make you feel special, wouldn't it? But you may want to be sure that the friend didn't miss anything, so why not go straight to the source?

The thing about God is He never changes. *"Jesus Christ [is] the same yesterday, and today, and forever"* (Hebrews 13:8 KJV). So you don't have to worry about Him changing; He will not. We are the ones who change, and we think that we are showing Him something by not worshipping Him in spirit and truth.

"For my thoughts are not your thoughts, neither are your ways my ways, saith the Lord. For as the heavens are higher than the earth, so are my ways higher than your ways, and my thoughts than your thoughts" (Isaiah 55:8-9, KJV).

Now don't cry too hard; see, you are just praying for Him to pay your rent when He wants you to own the entire complex.

Delight yourself in the Lord.

You were praying for the medicine to work, but He has already healed your body. Stop praying for Him to give you enough for one more car payment. Don't you know that He can afford to pay it off completely? He just wants unconditional praise rather than conditional probability praise (in other words, "Lord, the bills are paid, so I can praise you now"). No, that is not right.

"Verily verily I say unto you, the servant is not greater than his lord, neither he that is sent greater than he that sent him" (John 13:16, KJV). If Jesus endured such harsh conditions, what makes us think that our lives will be walks in the park? We will all suffer persecution, trials and tribulations, but we must count it all as joy.

Go ahead. Praise and worship Him until you can't praise and worship anymore. The Lord already knows when your tribulations will start and when they will end. *"For I know the thoughts that I think toward you, saith the Lord, thoughts of peace, and not of evil, to give you an expected end"* (Jeremiah 29:11, KJV).

Chapter

2

the true worshipper

These people draw near unto me with their mouth, and honor me with their lips, but their heart is far from me.
(Matt15:8)

When we worship and praise God in spirit and truth,
He knows it:

> *"If we have forgotten the name of our God or
> stretched out our hands to a strange god; shall not
> God search this out for he knoweth the secrets of
> the heart"*
> (Psalm 44:20-21, KJV)

What other god have you fallen captive to? What strange
god do you serve? Any material thing can become a strange
god, even people; then, before you know it, you are captive
to the something or someone other than the one, true God.

God is looking for the true worshipper. He is looking for
the one who, like Job, says, *"Though he slay me, yet will I trust
in him but I will maintain mine own ways before him. He also
shall by my salvation for an hypocrite shall not come before him"*
(Job 13:15-16, KJV).

A hypocrite is a person who puts on a false appearance of
virtue or religion; it is a person who acts in direct
contradiction to his or her stated beliefs. So, when someone
"worships" God with their mind set on material gain instead

of His face and His kingdom, they are a hypocrite. And according to Job, they shall not stand before Him. God is a spirit and you must reach into the spiritually realm in order to praise God.

God says in Revelation 3:16: "*So then because thou art lukewarm, and neither cold nor hot, I will spew thee out of my mouth.*" The Lord does not want your conditional probability praise. Have you ever had a glass of ice-cold milk? Its crisp coldness makes it pleasant. By contrast, a cup of hot milk is delicious because it is hot all the way through. But have you ever had a glass of room-temperature, lukewarm milk? It may start off cold but have spots of inconsistent warmness throughout. It is not committed to hot or cold, and the ambiguity is off-putting.

Romans 8:27 says, "*And he that searcheth the heart knoweth what is the mind of the spirit*" (KJV). This tells us that God searches our hearts, and He knows the true reasons behind your praise and worship.

God will test you only to give you a testimony of His goodness and love. I do believe in sweat-less victories, but I also know that the Word says that the servant is not above the master. This means that if Jesus suffered persecution, so will we. A true worshipper will praise God in the midst of any circumstances, no matter how trying. If your income check came short, and you only have enough money to pay your bills or your tithe, would you really have to stop and think about which one you would pay? Or do you believe that God will do what His Word says? God is looking for the radical people who know His Word and will do just what it says.

When God gave the Israelites the Ten Commandments, He said, *"Thou shalt not bow down thyself to any other God, nor serve them: for I the Lord thy God am a jealous God"* (Deuteronomy 5:9). Then, in the book of Daniel, we see three men stand on their faith in God's Word:

> "Nebuchadnezzar the king made an image of gold, whose height was threescore cubits and the breadth thereof six cubits: he set it up in the plain of Dura, in the province of Babylon.
>
> Then Nebuchadnezzar the king sent to gather together the princes, the governors and the captains, the judges, the treasurers, the counselors, the sheriffs and all the rulers of the provinces, to come to the dedication of the image that Nebuchadnezzar the king had set up...

Delight yourself in the Lord.

Then a herald cried aloud, to you it is commanded, O people, nations, and languages,

That at what time ye hear the sound of the cornet, flute, harp, sackbut, psaltery, dulcimer, and all kinds of music, ye fall down and worship the golden image that Nebuchadnezzar the king had set up.

And whoso falleth not down and worshippeth shall the same hour be cast into the midst of a burning fiery furnace...

Wherefore at that time certain Chaldeans came near, and accused the Jews.

They spake and said to the king Nebuchadnezzar, O king live forever. Thou, O king, hast made a decree, that every man that shall hear the sound of the cornet, flute, harp, sackbut, psaltery and dulcimer, and all kinds of music shall fall down and worship the golden image: And whoso falleth not down and worshippeth, that he should be cast into the midst of a burning fiery furnace. There are certain Jews whom thou hast set over the affairs of the province of Babylon, Shadrach, Meshach, and Abednego; these men, O king, have not regarded thee: they serve not thy gods, nor worship the golden image which thou hast set up.

Then Nebuchadnezzar in his rage and fury commanded to bring Shadrach, Meshach and Abednego. Then they brought these men before the king.

Nebuchadnezzar spake and said unto them, do not ye serve my gods nor worship the golden image which I have set up? Now if ye be ready that at what time ye hear the sound of the cornet, flute, harp, sackbut, psaltery and dulcimer, and all kinds of music, ye fall down and worship the image which I have made; well: but if ye worship not ye shall be cast the same hour into the midst of a burning fiery furnace; and who is that God that shall deliver you out of my hands?

Shadrach, Meshach, and Abednego, answered and said to the king, O Nebuchadnezzar, we are not careful to answer thee in this matter [in other words, they have no need to answer, for they are sure God will answer for them]. If it be so, our God whom we serve is able to deliver us from the burning fiery furnace, and he will deliver us out of thine hand, O king. But if not, be it known unto thee, O king, that we will not serve thy gods, nor worship the golden image which thou hast set-up.

Then was Nebuchadnezzar full of fury, and the form of his visage was changed against Shadrach, Meshach and Abednego: therefore he spake, and commanded that they should heat the furnace one seven times more than it was to be heated.

And the mightiest men that were in his army to bind Shadrach, Meshach, and Abednego, and to cast them into the burning fiery furnace.

Then these men were bound in their coats, their hosen, and their hats, and their other garments, and were cast into the midst of the burning fiery furnace.

Therefore because the king's commandment was urgent, and the furnace exceeding hot, the flames of the fire slew those men that took up Shadrach, Meshach, and Abednego. And these three men Shadrach, Meshach, and Abednego, fell down bound into the midst of the burning fiery furnace.

Then Nebuchadnezzar the king was astonished, and

rose up in haste, and spake, and said unto his counselors, did not we cast three men bound into the midst of the fire? They answered and said unto the king, True, O king.

He answered and said, Lo, I see four men loose, walking in the midst of the fire, and they have no hurt; and the form of the fourth is like the Son of God.

Then Nebuchadnezzar came near to the mouth of the burning fiery furnace, and spake, and said, Shadrach, Meshach, and Abednego, ye servants of the most high God, come forth, and come hither. Then Shadrach, Meshach, and Abednego, came forth of the midst of the fire.

And the princes, governors, and captains, and the king's counselors, being gathered together, saw these men, upon whose bodies the fire had no power, nor was an hair of their head singed, neither were their coats changed, nor the smell of fire had passed on them.

Then Nebuchadnezzar spake, and said, Blessed be the God of Shadrach, Meshach, and Abednego, who hath sent his angel, and delivered his servants that trusted in him, and have changed the king's word, and yielded their bodies, that they might not serve nor worship any god, except their own God.

Therefore I make a decree, That every people, nation, and language, which speak anything amiss against the God of Shadrach, Meshach, and Abednego, shall be cut in pieces, and their houses shall be made a dunghill: because there is no other God that can deliver after this sort.

Then the king promoted Shadrach, Meshach, and Abednego, in the province of Babylon (Daniel 3:1-2, 4-6, 8-30).

We serve a God who gave us free will. You should praise and worship God because you love Him, even if He does nothing else for you. He sent His Son to die for us, He gave us salvation, and He lavishes benefits on us daily. Because of their trust, unconditional praise and obedience, God delivered Shadrach, Meshach, and Abednego and promoted them. Even their enemy was persuaded to praise God as a result of their faith. These are the true worshippers God seeks. When you are in the fire, trust God; He is willing and able to deliver you.

Let Jesus' words be of comfort: "*Therefore take no thought, saying, what shall we eat? Or, what shall we drink? Or, Wherewithal shall we be clothed? (For after all these things do the Gentiles seek :) for your heavenly Father knoweth that ye have need of all these things. But seek ye first the kingdom of god, and his righteousness; and all these things shall be added unto you"* (Matthew 6:31-33, KJV).

"The silver is mine, and the gold is mine, saith the Lord of hosts" (Haggai 2:8, KJV). We serve a God of infinite abundance. If all wealth belongs to Him, will He not fulfill all of your needs and desires? We think we have God figured out, but we don't trust Him enough to praise Him regardless of our circumstances.

Praise invites and facilitates the manifestation of God's presence, so we also know that praise repels the enemy. Never let the atmosphere or any circumstances stop you from giving God the unconditional praise that is due to Him. He loves you so much, and you have His undivided attention. If you want to position yourself for God to radically move in your life (and make the devil really mad), just praise God unconditionally.

Jesus said, *"Behold the fowls of the air: for they sow not, neither do they reap, nor gather into barns; yet your heavenly Father feedeth*

Delight yourself in the Lord.

them. *Are ye not much better than they?"* (Matthew 6:26, KJV). We have something that the birds don't have, which I like to call a divine apparatus: a mouth. Use your mouth to praise the Lord your God. He is worthy to be praised.

In my neighborhood – well, in most neighborhoods – the birds get up early. I mean, I hear them cheerfully chirping outside my window at 4:00 a.m. I once asked my mother what they were doing, and she told me that they were just praising God.

See, even the birds know that they do not need to worry about what they will eat. By giving God praise, the ground is tilled for seeds of breakthrough in your life.

Chapter

3

unselfish praise

Praise and worship should be all about God, not about us. Never praise God because you want to bargain with Him for personal gain. If you sincerely seek His face,

> *"He shall give you the desires of your heart"*
> (Psalm 37:4, NKJV)

In the Old Testament, God said to Samuel, *"The Lord does not see as man sees; for a man looks at the outward appearance, but the Lord looks at the heart"* (1 Samuel 16:7). Don't think that you can keep a secret from God. With our natural eyes, we may see someone praising and worshiping God, but the heart God sees could be very different.

"Let them shout for joy, and be glad, that favor my righteous cause: yea, let them say continually, Let the Lord be magnified, which hath pleasure in the prosperity of his servants. And my tongue shall speak of thy righteousness and thy praise all the day long" (Psalm 35:27-28, KJV).

If you read that scripture with understanding, you will see that the Lord takes pleasure in the prosperity of His servants. So serve Him with praise, and He will take care of all your needs and bless you moreover. God is not cheap or stingy; He is abundant to no end.

Delight yourself in the Lord.

"To magnify" means "to make greater; to cause; to be held in greater esteem or respect" (Webster's Dictionary). When we magnify the Lord, we make Him greater than any problem, any bill, any health issue and anyone we face. God is worthy to be magnified. *"Ah Lord God! behold, thou hast made the heaven and the earth by thy great power and stretched out arm, and there is nothing too hard for thee"* (Jeremiah 32:17, KJV).

"Behold, I am the Lord, the God of all flesh: is there anything too hard for me?" (Jeremiah 32:27, KJV) No, there is nothing and no one greater or bigger than God!

When you pray, do you focus your prayers on your needs and the needs of your family and friends? Remember to pray for the man or woman you saw who was in trouble. Pray for your nation and your world, for spiritual leadership as well as government leadership, and for anyone in need. There are so many people in need right now; we can't afford to turn to the world system. God's kingdom is the best place to invest your praise, your trust and your money, for He will never go bankrupt or swindle you out of your inheritance.

What if you prayed for tribulations to stop, and God said, "No, I will not stop it, but if you endure it until the end, I will bless you."? God gives us tests to give us opportunities to trust Him; then He gives us testimonies of His faithfulness. There may be those who read this book who do not even believe that God exists, but how can He come through for you if you have never accepted His Son or praised Him? Make your tests turn into testimonies; give God the praise due Him, and help someone who may be lost. Give them a testimony by praising God in advance for someone else's breakthrough.

Ruth was one of the most selfless women in the Bible. If you are unfamiliar with her story, I encourage you to turn to the Book of Ruth in your Bible and read it; the whole book is only four chapters long. In the context of that book, what kind of person are you? Do you stick with God no matter the forecast or the diagnosis? How faithful is your praise and worship? Can you tell the Lord as Ruth told Naomi?

> *"Entreat me not to leave thee, or to return from following after thee: for whiter thou goest, I will go; and where thou lodgest, I will lodge: thy people shall be my people, and thy God my God: Where thou diest, will I die, and there will I be buried: the Lord do so to me, and more also, if ought but death part thee and me"* (Ruth 1:16-17, KJV).

If you continue to read, you will discover that after her

Delight yourself in the Lord.

return to Bethlehem, Naomi changes her name to Mara, which means bitterness. Like so many of us, she failed to see that the Lord never left her. But God knew that because of the death of her husband and two sons, Naomi needed someone faithful, so He provided Ruth.

Bitterness blinds you to blessings and hinders you from praising and worshiping God. In bitterness over what happen has happened or what has been lost, you cannot see the faithfulness of a loving God. He is able (and wants to) to restore you to better than ever before. I encourage you to praise and worship your way out of difficult situations. When you magnify the Lord, you won't dwell on pain and fear until you swell with bitterness. Let it go. Stop giving in to pity parties; God is on the move. Are you going with Him, or are you staying stagnant in bitterness?

Later in the story, because of Ruth's faithfulness and selflessness, she marries Boaz, a wealthy man who was actually kin to Naomi. Boaz knew of Ruth's faithfulness, and he showed her favor by commanding his young men to let her have some of the barley. *"And Boaz answered and said unto her, It hath fully been showed me, all that thou hast done unto thy mother in law since the death of thine husband: and how thou hast left thy father and mother, and the land of thy nativity, and art* come unto a people which thou knewest not heretofore" (Ruth 2:11, KJV).

What are you willing to leave for God? What have you been so wrapped up in that you can't praise and worship the Lord? What is stopping you from faithfully praising Him? What is making you so prideful that you won't humble yourself and give your highest praise to the Most High?

What is the motive of your praise and worship to God? Are you trying to gain something for yourself, or do you seek to lose yourself and gain Christ? When we are willing to give something up in order to be faithful to God, we set ourselves up to be blessed by the Lord of recompense.

"He that loveth his life shall lose it; and he that hateth his life in this world shall keep it unto life eternal. If any man serve me, let him follow me; and where I am, there shall also my servant be: if any man serve me, him will my Father honor" (John 12:25-26, KJV).

"The Lord recompense thy work, and a full reward be given thee of the Lord God of Israel, under whose wings thou art come to trust" (Ruth 2:12, KJV).

We all want God to pour out our full reward on us as soon

Delight yourself in the Lord.

as trials and tribulations end. Unconditional praise and worship with right motives will surely bring you into the presence of God, and *"in the presence is fullness of joy; at thy right hand there are pleasures for evermore"* (Psalm 16:11, KJV).

When an army of soldiers go to battle, they carry specialized weapons with which they can skillfully defeat their enemy. God created praise to be a mighty weapon against demonic forces.

(Psalm 22:3KJV) *says that God inhabits the praises of His people.* As we praise Him, we place Him on a throne as Lord over our lives, and the enemy is rendered powerless against us. That's why the devil does everything he can to keep you from praising God; the devil can't dwell where there is praise and worship to God.

When Paul and Silas praised God in prison in Acts 16:25-26, the doors opened and they escaped.

Praise lifts us out of our self-centered ways and repels the forces of evil. The power of praise helps us to focus on God and realize our need for Him. When we recognize His authority and faithfulness, God will bring victory. This makes praise, prayer and dependence on God a great weapon in spiritual warfare. No matter what appears to be going on in your natural world, praise the Lord. He seeks unconditional praise.

"And now my head shall be lifted up above my enemies all around me; Therefore I will offer sacrifices of joy in His tabernacle; I will sing, yes, I will sing praises to the Lord" (Psalm 27:6, KJV)

Look at how the word "praise" is spelled: The end is "raise" which means, "to lift up higher." How awesome it was when the Lord revealed this to me! Praise is the means by which God reveals Himself to His people! Praise God unconditionally and unselfishly.

Delight yourself in the Lord.

Chapter

4

the prosperity of fools

"He that walketh with wise men shall be wise: but a companion of fools shall be destroyed"
(Proverbs 13:20, KJV)

Who are your friends? Are there foolish people in your circle of friends? Do you associate with people who get their wealth by cheating others? God has already provided for us, His children, to have plenty. To gain wealth foolishly is the prosperity of fools.

You may think I've gotten off-topic, but you and your children will be blessed according to your unconditional praise. When people think they are smarter than their Creator, they can only gain the prosperity of fools. There can be no creation without a creator. Paul warned the Romans about ungodly men,

"Who changed the truth of God into a lie and worshipped and served the creature more than the creator" (Romans 1:25, KJV).

Worship the Lord in spirit and truth. Be faithful with your praise, but not because you want to get something from God.

Delight yourself in the Lord.

"And the wealth of a sinner is laid up for the just" (Proverbs 13:22, KJV).

Yes, amen. Praise the Lord! So you see, it is not worth living a self-righteous life. God will bring justice for His honest people. We have already seen this happen in the Bible, and it will happen again. If you study the Bible on this subject, you will find faithfulness, honor and praise to God in godly men. Each time God's people obeyed Him; there was a transfer of wealth to them at the expense of the wicked. Here are some examples:

> Joseph in Egypt (Genesis 47:13-26): *Through seven years of great prosperity followed by seven years of great famine, the wealth of Egypt was laid in the hands of an Israelite. Joseph was sold into slavery by his own brothers, but he was faithful to praise God and to fulfill God's will. See, sometimes God will put you in a place that seems unnecessarily harsh or unfair, only to reposition you for leadership. Joseph went from being a slave to being a ruler in Egypt.*

> Israel's exodus from Egypt (Exodus 7:12, 14 & 12:36): *After ten plagues from God, the Egyptians gave the people of Israel their freedom.*

<u>Four lepers and the army of Syria</u> (2 Kings 7): *God caused the army of Syria to hear a noise of horses, chariots and great host which caused the army to flee. They left behind enough wealth to bring Israel out of an economic depression and a famine in one day.*

<u>Judah is delivered from the armies of three nations</u> (2 Chronicles 20:1-25): *When God's people worshipped Him on the battlefield, He supernaturally caused the armies against them to destroy one another. It took them three days to carry away all of the wealth they gained because it was so great.*

<u>King Solomon's wealth</u> (1 Kings 10:13-27 & 2 Chronicles 9:13-27): *Solomon accumulated so much gold during his reign that the silver was not even counted among Israel's riches. God has said that He will rebuild the tabernacle of David (Acts 15:16, Amos 9:11, Isaiah 16:5). This includes wealth as well as worship.*

So you see, God knows how to bring you out of any situation. Foolishly pursuing prosperity does not profit you at all, for God is just. It is not worth losing God to gain riches. Resist cravings for material gain, but hunger for God all the more, and worship and praise Him in spirit and

Delight yourself in the Lord.

truth. When you accept Jesus Christ and follow His will, your purpose is no longer just a job with a set of gifts; it turns into an anointing. Here are some reference points of God's judgment on the wicked rich in the Bible:

(Ezekiel 7:19, KJV): *They shall cast their silver in the streets, and their gold shall be removed: their silver and their gold shall not be able to deliver them in the day of the wrath of the Lord...because it is the stumbling block of their iniquity.*

(James 5:1-7 KJV): *Go to now, ye rich men, weep and howl for your miseries that shall come upon you. Your riches are corrupted, and your garments are moth eaten. Your gold and silver is cankered; and the rust of them shall be a witness against you, and shall eat your flesh as it were fire. Ye have heaped treasure together for the last days. Behold, the hire of the laborers who have reaped down your fields, which is of you kept back by fraud crieth: and the cries of them which have reaped are entered into the ears of the Lord of Sabbath.*

(God has allowed the wicked to accumulate all kinds of treasure for His use in the last days. This goes back to Proverbs 13:22.)

(Deuteronomy 8:17-18, KJV): *And thou say in thine heart, my power and might of mine hand hath gotten me this wealth. But thou shalt remember the Lord thy God: for it is he that giveth thee power to get wealth that he may establish his covenant.* [Many foolish people fail to realize that money has a mission in the earth: to go into the entire world and establish God's covenant of love, blessing, kindness, mercy and peace. Nothing missing, nothing broken.]

(Ecclesiastes 2:26, Amp): *For to the person who pleases him God gives wisdom and knowledge and joy; but to the sinner he gives the work of gathering and heaping up, that he may give to one who pleases God.*

The prosperity of the foolish will be justly distributed among the faithful, to the glory of God. Though you experience tribulations, it is only for the glory of God. Praise Him, receive His Son, and you won't suffer consequences of foolishly gaining wealth.

"Thou hast caused men to ride over our heads; we went through fire and through water: but thou broughtest us out into a wealthy place" (Psalm 66:12, KJV).

Delight yourself in the Lord.

Trust and believe God. Praise and worship Him unconditionally. He loves us all unconditionally, and He is truly worthy to be praised unconditionally.

Chapter

5

faithless generation

Some people praise and worship God but rarely see Him move in their lives. Their praise is tied to conditions, and they won't glorify God unless they think personal gain will result. But God created us with free will – the ability to choose whether we serve Him or not. We all have a choice.

But if your [mind and] heart turn away and you will not hear, but are drawn away to worship other gods and serve them, I declare to you today that you shall surely perish, and you shall not live long in the land which you pass over the Jordan to enter and possess.

"I call heaven and earth to witness this day against you that I have set before you life and death, the blessings and the curses; therefore choose life, that you and your descendants may live" (Deuteronomy 30:17-19, Amp)

In Chapter One of this book, I outlined John 4:23-24: *"But the hour cometh, and now is, when the true worshippers shall worship the Father in spirit and in truth: for the Father seeketh such to worship him. God is a spirit: and they that worship him must worship him in spirit and in truth"* (KJV).

Delight yourself in the Lord.

If you do not approach the Spirit of God humbly, wanting the Creator more than any part of creation, then you will miss out on the awesome presence of God. In the presence of God are unparalleled love, peace, joy, rest and safety. When I am in the presence of the Lord, there is nothing in the world that can compare to the fullness of His presence.

People of little faith will try to swindle anyone and everyone – even God – because they are operating in fear. Fear is the opposite of faith, *"For God hath not given us the spirit of fear; but of power, and of love, and of a sound mind"* (2 Timothy 1:7, KJV).

Proverbs 3:25 says, *"Be not afraid of sudden fear, neither of desolation of the wicked, when it cometh"* (KJV).

Through His Word, God tells us never to fear, so we are free to give Him our unconditional praise. Don't wait; praise Him for victories you have yet to see; the battle has already been won, and you have a guaranteed victory in Jesus Christ. It is already yours!

Fear is a lie. Its only purpose is to cause us to doubt the promises of God and thus draw us away from Him. To fight the fear of the unknown, counteract it with faith that is firmly rooted in what is known: the faithfulness of God. The

Amplified Bible says that *"faith is the assurance... of the things [we] hope for, being the proof of things [we] do not see and the conviction of their reality"* (Hebrews 11:1). The verse goes on to say that faith perceives *"as real fact what is not revealed to the senses"* (Amp). Don't become a part of a faithless generation that operates in fear because they have little faith in His Word.

"I called upon the Lord in distress: the Lord answered me, and set me in a large place. The Lord is on my side; I will not fear: what can man do unto me?" (Psalm 118:5-6, KJV).

Faith shows the enemy that you have confidence in the Lord; and he is powerless against a child of God who knows their Father.

In Matthew 17, there was a man whose son was possessed by an evil spirit, and this caused the boy to throw himself into fire and water. His father had tried to take him to Jesus' disciples, but they could not cure him or cast out the demonic spirit. Look what Jesus said:

"O Faithless and perverse generation, how long shall I be with you? How long shall I suffer you? Bring him hither to me" (Matthew 17:17, KJV). After Jesus cast the spirit out of the

Delight yourself in the Lord.

boy, His disciples approached Him, asking, "Why could not we cast him out? And Jesus said unto them, Because of your unbelief: for verily I say unto you, if ye have faith as a grain of mustard seed, ye shall say unto this mountain, Remove hence to yonder place; and it shall remove; and nothing shall be impossible unto you. Howbeit this kind goeth not out but by prayer and fasting" (Matthew 17:19-21, KJV).

Fasting is a consistent form of praise and worship to the Lord; when you fast, you are saying to God, "I want you more than the things of this world." Some trials and tribulations may require fasting as our praise and worship. If you fast for three full days, your life has continuously been an offering of praise to God for three days. If someone were to come and sit in your face for three days, staring at you without movement, that would surely get your attention. Fasting is a consistent praise to God it causes use to focus, but you must approach it with the right motives, the right heart and the right mindset. If you fast and don't hear from God clearly after the fast is over, you may need to check your motive for fasting.

Unconditional praise and worship is very important; God loves us so much, and the enemy always uses what you love as a weapon against you. But God has given us a weapon of praise and we are fully equipped to fight against the devil and demonic forces.

Jesus said, *"Verily I say unto you, whatever ye shall bind on earth shall be bound in heaven: and whatsoever ye shall loose on earth shall be loosed in heaven"* (Matthew 18:18, KJV). When you let loose your praise and worship on earth, it is loosed in heaven as well.

The Lord has told us that all we need is faith as small as a mustard seed to achieve the impossible, but of course we, the microwave generation, want everything now. To us, it may seem like Job suffered pain and loss for years, but it was only nine months before God restored his health and family and blessed him with more than he started with. The Lord honored Job's faith and took away his suffering.

In the midst of trials and tribulations, nine months may seem like a very long time, but God only sends the fire to burn up the things that are binding you. Make your tribulations holy ground; in times of trouble, summon heaven. Every time is a good time to praise God, but when tribulation comes, there is something extra special about unconditional praise.

Delight yourself in the Lord.

How many of us can speak as Job did in (Job 13:15), *"Though he slay me, yet will I trust in him"* (KJV)? Or, because of your faithlessness, do you speak as Job's wife did: *"Dost thou still retain thine integrity? Curse God, and die"* (Job 2:9, KJV).

Remember, there is nothing too difficult for God. Though you may wonder when your breakthrough will come, know the Word of God, believe it, praise Him and seek Him for answers. Search the Word, and don't faint. Stand firm on the Word of the Lord.

"For my thoughts are not your thoughts, neither are your ways my ways, saith the Lord" (Isaiah 55:8, KJV).

This tells us that God is not like us; He knows when your tribulation will end, so praise Him right in the middle of it, and count it all as joy, for all things work together for the good of those who love the Lord (Romans 8:28). Hard times can only work for your benefit, so give God your unconditional praise.

Praise be to God always and forever. He won't resign, and no one can impeach Him. Glory to God.

"For I am God and there is no one else" (Isaiah 45:22, KJV)

Chapter

seek first

In Matthew 6, Jesus said,

"Therefore I say unto you, take no thought, saying, what shall we eat? or, What shall we drink? or, Wherewithal with shall we be clothed? (For after all these things do the gentiles seek :) for your heavenly Father knoweth that ye have need of all these things. But seek ye first the kingdom of God, and his righteousness; and all these things shall be added unto you"
(Matthew 6:31-33, KJV)

God's Word clearly says to seek the kingdom of God and His righteousness first, and He will supply all of your needs. We must seek God fervently, passionately. When we seek God and find Him that is pure delight. Don't you think our awesome God knows what you need? He knows what you need before you ask Him; He knew you before you were formed in your mother's womb, and He knows the pleasure of your wants as well.

Delight yourself in the Lord.

As I said in Chapter One, God wants your unconditional praise; this point is worth repeating. You cannot praise God in spirit and truth while being disobedient. Praising God while harboring bitterness, malice and unforgiveness toward others is hypocrisy. How can you love God when you won't forgive those who have offended you? We are supposed to love God with all of our hearts, with all of our souls and with all of our strength (Deuteronomy 6:5). There are the many ways to honor God, including tithing, giving, fasting, praying, praising and worshipping. We have become so consumed with pride and selfishness that no one else matters, not even God. His Word does not carry weight in our lives like it is meant to.

In 2 Chronicles, Solomon praised God with his giving. By his offerings to God, He let the Lord and everyone in the region know that everything he had came from the Lord. Solomon gave from his heart unselfishly, not caring whether God would increase his wealth or not.

And Solomon went up thither to the brazen alter before the Lord, which was at the tabernacle of the congregation, and offered a thousand burnt offerings upon it. In that night did God appear unto Solomon, and said unto him, Ask what I shall give thee. And Solomon said unto God, Thou hast showed great mercy unto David my father, and hast made me to reign in his stead. Now, O Lord God, let thy promise into David my father be established: for thou hast made me king over a people like a dust of the earth in multitude. Give me now wisdom and knowledge that I may go out and come in before this people: for who can judge this thy people that is so great? And God said to Solomon, Because this was in thine heart, and thou hast not asked riches, wealth, or honor, nor the life of thine enemies, neither yet hast asked long life; but hast asked wisdom and knowledge for thyself, that thou mayest judge my people, over whom I have made thee king: Wisdom and knowledge is granted unto thee; and I will give thee riches, and wealth, and honor, such as none of the kings have had that have been before thee, neither shall there any after thee have the like (2 Chronicles 1:6-12).

In his God-given wisdom, Solomon wrote, *"Wisdom is the principal thing; therefore get wisdom: and with all thy getting get understanding"* (Proverbs 4:7, KJV). I include scriptures in this book for understanding; without any understanding of God's Word, it is useless.

King Solomon asked God to give him the wisdom to manage what he already had; he did not ask out of greed or selfishness. And because God saw his heart to serve

Delight yourself in the Lord.

unconditionally, God granted him more than what he asked for; He gave him wisdom with which to judge his people and blessed him with unprecedented wealth. But Solomon first gave God unconditional praise through his offerings. He never tied his giving to whether or not the Lord would give him more riches. In a parable, Jesus showed God's response to our faithfulness: *"Well done, good and faithful servant; thou hast been faithful over few things, I will make thee ruler over many things: enter thou into the joy of thy lord"* (Matthew 25:23, KJV). We often pray for God to increase our wealth, but Psalm 138:8 says that He will perfect that which concerns you. Giving God your unconditional praise and worship will magnify Him. No matter what you are facing, God is using it to better you. We must die to our own wills and say yes to His will every day. If you want to know the will of God, read His Word, for His will has been already set: *"All scripture is given by inspiration of God, and is profitable for doctrine, for reproof, for correction, for instruction in righteousness"* (2 Timothy 3:16, KJV).

This verse tells us that scripture is inspired by God; in others words, it came from His mouth. The Word is full of His thoughts and ways, and if you do what it says in righteousness, your results will be good. At the end of 2 Timothy 3:16, we see the word "righteousness," which means "doing what is right." If you are praying for financial increase but you are not tithing, I would encourage you to give cheerfully and bank on God's faithfulness. If you are making $30,000 a year but you are not tithing, why would you tithe if you were to get $100 million? As I said in Chapter Four, money has a purpose on earth. We are blessed to be a blessing, and "blessed" implies an empowerment to succeed. So, if your purpose is to bless others, then you can stop misfortune in the lives of others. This is why we must seek first the Lord and His kingdom. When we seek the Lord, He will show us who we really are. Do you really want the Lord, or just His stuff?

Jesus said, *"For you say, I am rich; I have prospered and grown wealthy, and I am in need of nothing; and you do not realize and understand that you are wretched, pitiable, poor, blind, and naked"* (Revelation 3:17, Amp).

Bishop T.D. Jakes once said, *"Resources without strategy lead to poverty."* You think you are something great, but without the Lord, your soul is naked.

"Glory ye in his holy name: let the heart of them rejoice that seek the Lord. Seek the Lord and his strength, seek his face continually" (1 Chronicles 16:10-11, KJV). This means every day.

Delight yourself in the Lord.

"Thou wilt show me the path of life: in thy presence is fullness of joy; at thy right hand there are pleasures for evermore" (Psalm 16:11, KJV).

We just need to praise God and trust Him to provide for us in abundance. When we seek the Lord and praise Him in the middle of tribulations, He will honor our trust in Him.

"Who shall separate us from the love of Christ? shall tribulation, or distress, or persecution, or famine, or nakedness, or peril, or sword?" (Romans 8:35, KJV).

This is the question the enemy tries to answer every day of our lives. He wants to know how he can separate us from the love of Christ.

"And I give unto them eternal life; and they shall never perish, neither shall any man pluck them out of my hand" (John 10:28, KJV).

The only way the enemy can cause separation is to keep you in sin. Sin separates us from God, but not from His love. God's love for us is unconditional and everlasting. This is why you should give God your unconditional praise; if you need a reason, there is no better one than the fact that He loves you and cares about you. When trouble arrives, make your situation a sanctuary. The Book of James says that faith without works is dead, so we all must do some work. Just start off with confession every day; use the Word of God to locate one of His promises. Then apply it to your life every day until you see the manifestation of what you have confessed, and don't ever give doubt a place in your mind. You must completely trust and rely on the Lord.

Jesus said, *"Ask, and it shall be given you; seek, and ye shall find; knock, and it shall be opened unto you: For everyone that asketh receiveth; and he that seeketh findeth; and to him that knocketh it shall be opened"* (Matthew 7:7-8, KJV). When you seek the Lord, He will and does hear and answer you.

Seek the Lord, and you will find Him. Praise and worship truthfully for no reason other than because you love and trust Him. No matter what happens, stand on the Word of God; praise and worship are the best gift God has given us, and they are His favorite gifts to receive.

"Therefore, my beloved brethren, be ye steadfast, unmovable, always abounding in the work of the Lord, forasmuch as ye know that your labor is not in vain in the Lord" (1 Corinthians 15:58, KJV).

Give God your unconditional praise by seeking first His

Delight yourself in the Lord.

kingdom and His righteousness. Knowing that it is not in vain, seek Him first with unconditional praise.

Chapter

7

he will supply

God will and is very able to take care of us. The problem is, as Jesus stated in Matthew 6:30,

"O ye of little faith."

Most Christians who know the Word have short bursts of faith. We tend to believe for a little while, but when we don't see instant results, we faint. God will supply. His Word is true. Of course we will have doubts, but don't confess everything that comes to your mind. It is up to you to abort any thought that contradicts what you know to be true about God's word from Scripture. The mind is the battleground for your victory.

"Now unto him that is able to do exceeding abundantly above all that we ask or think, according to the power that worketh in us, Unto him be glory" (Ephesians 3:20-21, KJV).

If you can imagine it, He can do exceedingly more. Praise gives kingdom access to all born-again believers; you must receive Jesus Christ and confess Him as your Lord and Savior. Our Heavenly Father did not leave us as orphans; He longs for His children to believe and give Him unconditional praise. He knows what we need; what kind of Father would He be if He didn't supply for you?

Delight yourself in the Lord.

"There hath no temptation taken you but such as is common to man: but God is faithful, who will not suffer you to be tempted above that ye are able; but will with the temptation also make a way to escape, that ye may be able to bear it" (1 Corinthians 10:13, KJV).

God is awesome! He makes a way for us to escape from every situation – every time. Following God's will won't lead us down a path to suicide, so don't think that this is the way of escape. It is not. But your praise is a way of escape, for when you praise God, you are in His presence, and there you will find help, peace and fullness of joy. Worship and praise are the way to the presence of God.

When your need arrived, what did you do first? Did you place God on the back burner in case everything and everyone else failed to fulfill you? God must be your source, not people, job, or self, but the Lord. In Chapter Six, I spoke about seeking first the kingdom, and He shall supply all your needs. Stop putting God seventh on the list; He will come through for you every time when He is put first. God's kingdom way always works; you must follow the instructions He gave us, which are in the Bible. God will supply.

Have you ever purchased something from the store that

needed to be assembled? I would bet that the manufacturer provided instructions, and if you followed those instructions, you would probably get it exactly right. But if you purchased an item, never read the instructions, and tried to put it together, it would probably be a long, confusing process. Well God bought us for a price; the blood of Jesus paid for us in full, and if we are going to walk around in circles and never read the manual He gave us, it is going to cost us many long, painful failures before we finally pick up the Word of God and read the instructions. *"Come unto me, all ye that labor and are heavy laden, and I will give you rest. Take my yoke upon you, and learn of me; for I am meek and lowly in heart: and ye shall find rest unto your souls. For my yoke is easy, and my burden is light"* (Matthew 11: 28-30, KJV).

If you don't read the Bible, you would not know that Jesus is calling all who are heavy-laden. When you need rest and try to find it elsewhere, you find no resting place because you are searching in all the wrong places. When you truly believe that God will provide for you, it makes it easy for you to give Him unconditional praise.

If the kingdom of God will work for you, you must renew your mind. As I said before, His will is His Word. There is

Delight yourself in the Lord.

a Trinity in the kingdom of God: the Father, the Son, and the Holy Spirit. Each does His part in the kingdom of God, just as we each have the opportunity to do our part: When we accept Christ, read the Bible, pray, praise unconditionally and believe, we are doing our part to glorify God.

"But we glory in tribulations also: knowing that tribulations worketh patience" (Romans 5:3, KJV).

"But let patience have her perfect work, that ye may be perfect and entire, wanting nothing" (James 1:4, KJV).

So, after praising God unconditionally, know that breakthrough may not come right away, but *"tribulations worketh patience." "And we know that all things work together for good to them that love God, to them who are the called according to his purpose"* (Romans 8:28, KJV).

Not in "some things," but in "all things" – so the lost job, the unforgiveness, the betrayal, the house foreclosure – in all things, God is developing you through His process. Don't faint; you are almost where He wants you to be. Remember His will, not yours.

"Being confident of this very thing, that he which hath begun a

good work in you will perform it until the day of Jesus Christ" (Philippians 1:6, KJV).

God is faithful to His Word. If you are serious about achieving spiritual maturity and experiencing the fullness of God in your life, you must be rooted and grounded in the Word of God and in love (Ephesians 3:17). This requires spending time reading His Word every day and trusting that no matter what afflictions and temptations arise, He has already made a way of escape for us. The enemy's plan is to keep you out of God's Word as much as possible. If you try reading the Word of God impatiently, don't let the enemy convince you that it doesn't work. Most of us never continue doing what we know to be true long enough to get results. For example, if you eat right and exercise for one month, then you will only see results for that length of time. Your weight loss will probably not be very great. Jesus said, *"If ye continue in my word, then are ye my disciples indeed; and ye shall know the truth, and the truth shall make you free"* (John 8:31-32, KJV). If we continue with the weight-loss example, then the truth is that weight loss needs to be achieved. This may be the truth, but if you do not practice the things that will help you lose weight, then what good is that truth? If you do nothing with your knowledge of the truth then you will remain unchanged.

Delight yourself in the Lord.

The devil can only make you feel tired and weary if you allow him to continue to speak lies. Don't give up. Here is a secret: The demons get tired too. Every time you hold fast to the Word of God and resist evil thoughts or plead the blood of Jesus against a nagging habit, you resist them. Every time you quote Scripture in the midst of tribulations, you are fighting back at them. To fight a spiritual battle, you must have a spiritual weapon, and God has supplied one for you. His Word is the sword of the Spirit. So much has and will come against you because the enemy is trying to make you tired. He often uses things that we love to hurt us, and he only wants you because he knows how much God loves you. He wants to hurt God by leading you into sin and keeping you blind. If he can do that, he can hinder the powerful weapons of praise and worship.

God is not trying to hide how you can have victory in every area of your life (health, debt, unforgiveness, love and anything else that concerns you). He can and will supply all that you need. If you never sow your time in the Word of God, how can you reap from it? Whatever we loose on earth will be loosed in heaven. The Lord has assigned His angels to us, that when the word of God flows from your mouth it has creative ability, the angels must hearken and bring into reality the promises of God which we spoke.

One morning, I was praising God as I was driving to work, and I finally said, "Lord, I give you my unconditional praise." And the Spirit of the Lord started to speak to me about His views on unconditional praise. He spoke clearly to me that your praise is the release button for the Lord to open His ears to your prayers. God wants His people to praise Him willingly and unconditionally. He longs for people who want no one more than Him, who hunger and thirst for nothing more than Him. We were created to praise Him and give Him unconditional praise without probability of success. God loves you so much. Let your unconditional praise rise to His ears and heart. Give Him your unconditional praise, and the Lord will do what His Word says now that you have completed this book, my prayer and supplication for you is that the chains that held you from trusting in God's word, that kept your from praising God anyway is now broken and you can really give him your Unconditional Praise.

Use your praise as your weapon, praise him right in the middle of all the hell and fire you are going through, I say to you today, God has sent the fiery trial that very thing you are battling to burn up the old so that you may receive the newness he has for you.

Delight yourself in the Lord.

This is a fixed fight and the battle is not yours but the lords, give him a shout of praise for no other reason but because you love him and you trust him.

"When the enemy shall come in like a flood, the Spirit of the Lord shall lift up a standard against him" (Isaiah 59:19, KJV). Give God unconditional praise!

Coming Soon

Better Not Bitter

What You See is Not What You Get

Receive

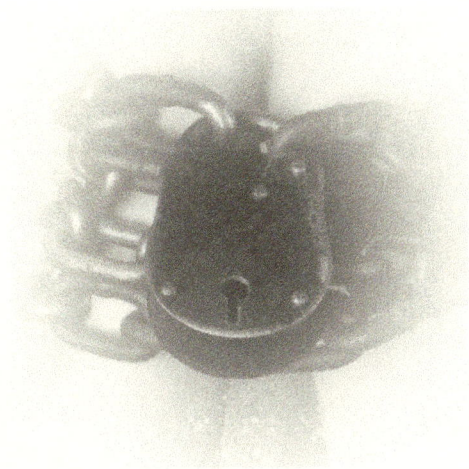

www.ingramcontent.com/pod-product-compliance
Lightning Source LLC
Chambersburg PA
CBHW020509100426
42813CB00030B/3166/J